Truelife Trivia

LeBron James

300 Trivia Questions and Fun Facts

BY BRYSEN HOLTZ

Truelife Trivia Series

Copyright ©2026 by Brysen Holtz All rights reserved. No part of this book may be used or reproduced in any manner whatsoever without the express written permission of the publisher except for the use of brief quotations in a book review

The author and publisher make no warranty, expressed or implied, that the information contained herein is appropriate for all individuals, situations or purposes, and assume no responsibility for errors or omission. The reader assumes the risk and full responsibility for all actions, and the authors will not be held liable for any loss or damage, whether consequential.

Truelife Trivia: LeBron James 300 Trivia Questions and Fun Facts. Truelife Trivia Series
Truelife Trivia an imprint of TLM Media LLC

ISBN-13: 979-8-88700-609-3

1. LeBron James wears which jersey number?

A. 6

B. 8

C. 10

D. 23

2. Critics admire his?

A. Longevity

B. Short peak

C. Decline

D. Retirement

3. LeBron James's demeanor is?

A. Loud

B. Confident

C. Reserved

D. Cheerful

4. LeBron active online via?

A. Posts

B. Silence

C. Absence

D. Retreat

5. LeBron James was a fan of?

A. Baseball
B. Football
C. Soccer
D. Basketball

6. LeBron James grew up watching which sport?

A. Basketball
B. Baseball
C. Football
D. Hockey

7. LeBron story starts in?

A. Big city
B. Small town
C. Abroad
D. Suburbs

8. LeBron James played which position in football?

A. Quarterback
B. Receiver
C. Running back
D. Linebacker

9. NBA peers see LeBron as?

A. Threat
B. Leader
C. Obstacle
D. Problem

10. His hometown fame grew due to?

A. Music
B. Art
C. Sports
D. Politics

11. LeBron James's birth city is?

A. Cleveland
B. Columbus
C. Akron
D. Dayton

12. LeBron James's ex-teammate is?

A. Dwyane Wade
B. Kobe Bryant
C. Chris Paul
D. Phil

13. LeBron James's first child is?

A. Bronny
B. Bryce
C. LeBron Jr.
D. Xavier

14. LeBron James's rival is?

A. Kobe Bryant
B. Dwyane Wade
C. Carmelo Anthony
D. Phil

15. LeBron James has won how many MVP awards?

A. 2
B. 3
C. 4
D. 5

16. LeBron James's first Finals MVP was in?

A. 2010
B. 2011
C. 2012
D. 2013

17. LeBron James's brother's name is?

A. Dru
B. Carmelo
C. Chris
D. He has none

18. LeBron James's first NBA title was with?

A. Heat
B. Cavs
C. Lakers
D. Spurs

19. LeBron was born in?

A. Cleveland
B. Akron
C. Columbus
D. Dayton

20. LeBron James loves?

A. Sushi
B. Pizza
C. Burgers
D. Pasta

21. Early talent was?

A. Hidden
B. Average
C. Exceptional
D. Ignored

22. LeBron James is appreciated for his?

A. Versatility
B. Humor
C. Directing
D. Acting

23. LeBron James has a fear of?

A. Spiders
B. Heights
C. Snakes
D. Flying

24. LeBron is also a?

A. Director
B. Producer
C. Author
D. Designer

25. LeBron James won back-to-back titles in?

A. 2011-2012
B. 2012-2013
C. 2013-2014
D. 2014-2015

26. LeBron James's favorite holiday is?

A. Christmas
B. Easter
C. Halloween
D. Thanksgiving

27. LeBron James had a public relationship with?

A. Savannah Brinson
B. Kate Hudson
C. Rihanna
D. Phil

28. LeBron James's favorite movie is?

A. Space Jam
B. Aladdin
C. Pocahontas
D. Phil

29. LeBron James rose to fame with?

A. Cavs
B. Heat
C. Lakers
D. Spurs

30. LeBron James is described as?

A. Quirky
B. Bold
C. Reserved
D. Grounded

31. LeBron marriage known for?

A. Drama
B. Stability
C. Silence
D. Distance

32. LeBron James is known for his?

A. Style
B. Sincerity
C. Commitment
D. Work ethic

33. LeBron James's favorite color is?

A. Red

B. Blue

C. Green

D. Black

34. LeBron plays mainly as?

A. Center

B. Guard

C. Coach

D. Forward

35. LeBron James was drafted by?

A. Lakers

B. Cavs

C. Heat

D. Bulls

36. LeBron James is respected for his?

A. Humility

B. Humor

C. Joy

D. Work ethic

37. LeBron James became the all-time leading scorer in?

A. 2021
B. 2022
C. 2023
D. 2024

38. LeBron James starred in which movie?

A. Space Jam
B. Hoosiers
C. Coach Carter
D. Blue Chips

39. LeBron James's presence is?

A. Commanding
B. Soft
C. Strong
D. Subtle

40. LeBron James's middle name is?

A. Raymond
B. Anthony
C. Michael
D. Ramon

41. LeBron James was named Athlete of the Year by?

A. ESPN
B. Time
C. Sports Illustrated
D. Forbes

42. LeBron James's NBA debut was in?

A. 2001
B. 2002
C. 2003
D. 2004

43. LeBron James learned to read at age?

A. 3
B. 4
C. 5
D. 6

44. LeBron James has a tattoo of?

A. A Lion
B. A Bird
C. A Wolf
D. A Crown

45. LeBron James was born under which Chinese zodiac?

A. Ox
B. Horse
C. Dragon
D. Rat

46. LeBron is praised for?

A. Skill
B. Neglect
C. Minimalism
D. Ordinary

47. LeBron James led the league in scoring in?

A. 2007
B. 2008
C. 2009
D. 2010

48. League respect comes from?

A. Age
B. Legacy
C. Noise
D. Popularity

49. LeBron James was raised in which city?

A. Columbus
B. Dayton
C. Akron
D. Cleveland

50. LeBron James's middle name is?

A. Raymond
B. Michael
C. Anthony
D. Ramon

51. LeBron James's playing style is?

A. Subtle
B. Dramatic
C. Aggressive
D. Fast

52. Commentators note his?

A. Low IQ
B. Basketball IQ
C. Noise
D. Chaos

53. LeBron James's persona is?

A. Subtle
B. Grounded
C. Calm
D. Commanding

54. LeBron career spans?

A. One decade
B. Two decades
C. Short run
D. College only

55. LeBron James's highest scoring game was?

A. 50
B. 60
C. 61
D. 62

56. LeBron James is often described as?

A. Innovative
B. Funny
C. Versatile
D. Dominant

57. LeBron childhood taught?

A. Comfort
B. Discipline
C. Wealth
D. Ease

58. LeBron interests include?

A. Wine collecting
B. Stamp trading
C. Chess cards
D. Coins

59. LeBron James was born during which year?

A. 1982
B. 1983
C. 1984
D. 1985

60. LeBron teammates value his?

A. Silence
B. Leadership
C. Distance
D. Control

61. LeBron James won his first title in?

A. 2010
B. 2011
C. 2012
D. 2013

62. LeBron James is admired for his?

A. Kindness
B. Humor
C. Commitment
D. Dedication

63. LeBron respects his?

A. Roots
B. Enemies
C. Silence
D. Distance

64. LeBron James's mother encouraged him to?

A. Sing
B. Dance
C. Act
D. Play sports

65. LeBron James was born in which hospital?

A. Cedars-Sinai

B. UCLA

C. Mount Sinai

D. Summa

66. LeBron James's favorite book is?

A. The Hobbit

B. Harry Potter

C. To Kill a Mockingbird

D. Phil

67. LeBron James is friends with?

A. Chris Paul

B. Carmelo Anthony

C. Kobe Bryant

D. Phil

68. LeBron James's birth state is?

A. Nevada

B. Texas

C. Arizona

D. Ohio

69. LeBron James's persona is?

A. Outspoken
B. Loud
C. Calm
D. Trendy

70. LeBron James won his first MVP in?

A. 2007
B. 2008
C. 2009
D. 2010

71. LeBron James's first dunk was at age?

A. 10
B. 12
C. 14
D. 15

72. LeBron James's performances are?

A. Subtle
B. Aggressive
C. Emotional
D. Dramatic

73. LeBron James was drafted by?

A. Cavs
B. Lakers
C. Heat
D. Spurs

74. LeBron mentors?

A. Veterans only
B. Young players
C. No one
D. Opponents

75. LeBron is seen as?

A. Legend
B. Novice
C. Ordinary
D. Average

76. LeBron adapted to?

A. New roles
B. Retirement
C. Silence
D. Coaching

77. Media praise LeBron for?

A. Luck
B. Age
C. Durability
D. Silence

78. LeBron known for?

A. Discipline
B. Laziness
C. Neglect
D. Randomness

79. LeBron impact remained?

A. Limited
B. Reduced
C. Strong
D. Unnoticed

80. LeBron James grew up in which neighborhood?

A. Beverly Hills
B. Hollywood Hills
C. Spring Hill
D. East Akron

81. Fun side shows his?

A. Human side
B. Distance
C. Coldness
D. Silence

82. LeBron milestone includes?

A. Early exit
B. Father son duo
C. Trade only
D. Injury

83. LeBron James's presence is often?

A. Cheerful
B. Excited
C. Calm
D. Mysterious

84. Fans admire LeBron James's?

A. Creativity
B. Humor
C. Commitment
D. Work ethic

85. Legacy milestones highlight?

A. Age
B. Impact
C. Silence
D. Distance

86. LeBron James's longest friendship is with?

A. Dwyane Wade
B. Carmelo Anthony
C. Chris Paul
D. Dru Joyce

87. Veteran role expanded his?

A. Mentorship
B. Isolation
C. Silence
D. Distance

88. LeBron James's favorite actor is?

A. Denzel Washington
B. Will Smith
C. Tom Cruise
D. Phil

89. People view him as?

A. Trailblazer
B. Follower
C. Average
D. Ordinary

90. LeBron James had a rivalry with?

A. Paul Pierce
B. Kobe Bryant
C. Dwyane Wade
D. Phil

91. LeBron James won his first NBA title in?

A. 2010
B. 2011
C. 2012
D. 2013

92. LeBron James was drafted in which year?

A. 2001
B. 2002
C. 2003
D. 2004

93. Personal life reflects?

A. Chaos
B. Focus
C. Disorder
D. Neglect

94. LeBron James's first coach was?

A. Doc Rivers
B. Paul Silas
C. Frank Walker
D. Phil

95. LeBron James's first team was?

A. Cavs
B. Heat
C. Lakers
D. Spurs

96. LeBron James's influence is?

A. Global
B. Local
C. Regional
D. National

97. LeBron crossed which scoring mark?

A. 20000
B. 30000
C. 40000
D. 25000

98. LeBron James was drafted by?

A. Bulls
B. Heat
C. Cavs
D. Lakers

99. LeBron James's first MVP was in?

A. 2007
B. 2008
C. 2009
D. 2010

100. LeBron milestone seasons show?

A. Drop
B. Stability
C. Confusion
D. Absence

101. LeBron James's childhood nickname was?

A. Bron
B. Bronny
C. King
D. Little Bron

102. LeBron James is seen as a?

A. Leader
B. Follower
C. Benchwarmer
D. Role player

103. LeBron James played with?

A. Dwyane Wade
B. Michael Jordan
C. Magic Johnson
D. Phil

104. He is famous for?

A. Basketball
B. Politics
C. Movies
D. Singing

105. LeBron James led the league in assists in?

A. 2017
B. 2018
C. 2019
D. 2020

106. LeBron James is close friends with?

A. Chris Paul
B. Kobe Bryant
C. Michael Jordan
D. Dwyane Wade

107. LeBron James's first name is?

A. Michael
B. Raymond
C. LeBron
D. Anthony

108. LeBron James was named All-Star MVP in?

A. 2006
B. 2007
C. 2008
D. 2009

109. LeBron James is also known as?

A. The King
B. The Prince
C. The Legend
D. The Man

110. LeBron fitness routine is?

A. Relaxed
B. Strict
C. Minimal
D. Random

111. Which team is linked to LeBron in 2025?

A. Heat
B. Bulls
C. Celtics
D. Lakers

112. LeBron James is described as?

A. Mysterious
B. Quirky
C. Innovative
D. Versatile

113. LeBron birthplace state?

A. Texas
B. Florida
C. Ohio
D. California

114. LeBron James's first car was a?

A. BMW
B. Ford
C. Toyota
D. Hummer

115. LeBron enjoys?

A. Cooking
B. Training
C. Knitting
D. Painting

116. LeBron rivals respect his?

A. Weakness
B. Experience
C. Noise
D. Luck

117. LeBron James's favorite player growing up?

A. Michael Jordan
B. Kobe Bryant
C. Magic Johnson
D. Larry Bird

118. LeBron avoids public?

A. Feuds
B. Support
C. Dialogue
D. Praise

119. LeBron legacy feels?

A. Lasting
B. Brief
C. Unclear
D. Temporary

120. LeBron James's first Finals MVP was in?

A. 2010
B. 2011
C. 2012
D. 2013

121. LeBron James's first All-Star MVP was in?

A. 2005
B. 2006
C. 2007
D. 2008

122. What is LeBron James last name?

A. Gaga
B. Julie
C. Hillary
D. James

123. LeBron James's current partner is?

A. Savannah Brinson
B. Kim Kardashian
C. BeyoncÃ©
D. Jennifer Lopez

124. LeBron James's favorite subject was?

A. Math
B. Science
C. History
D. English

125. LeBron business ventures include?

A. Fashion

B. Media

C. Politics

D. Real estate

126. LeBron James was born in which city?

A. Cleveland

B. Akron

C. Miami

D. Los Angeles

127. LeBron James was supported by?

A. Kobe Bryant

B. Chris Paul

C. Dwyane Wade

D. Phil

128. LeBron James was born during which season?

A. Summer

B. Fall

C. Winter

D. Spring

129. Career highs continued with?

A. Adaptation
B. Retreat
C. Absence
D. Injury

130. LeBron James's favorite food is?

A. Pizza
B. Pasta
C. Sushi
D. Burgers

131. LeBron roots connect to?

A. Miami
B. Akron
C. Chicago
D. Dallas

132. LeBron James is seen as?

A. Optimistic
B. Grounded
C. Innovative
D. Realistic

133. LeBron James's ex-teammate is?

A. Kobe Bryant
B. Chris Paul
C. Dwyane Wade
D. Phil

134. Family life keeps him?

A. Distracted
B. Grounded
C. Isolated
D. Absent

135. LeBron James's first scoring title was in?

A. 2007
B. 2008
C. 2009
D. 2010

136. LeBron off court passion?

A. Youth programs
B. Gambling
C. Fashion only
D. Travel

137. LeBron James's breakout year was?

A. 2001
B. 2002
C. 2003
D. 2004

138. LeBron James's first All-Star game was in?

A. 2004
B. 2005
C. 2006
D. 2007

139. Which sport defines LeBron?

A. Football
B. Tennis
C. Cricket
D. Basketball

140. LeBron James has worked with?

A. Kobe Bryant
B. Dwyane Wade
C. Chris Paul
D. Phil

141. LeBron James was criticized by?

A. Kobe Bryant
B. Paul Pierce
C. Carmelo Anthony
D. Phil

142. LeBron James became the face of which brand?

A. Adidas
B. Reebok
C. Nike
D. Puma

143. All time status earned by?

A. Hype
B. Stats
C. Consistency
D. Noise

144. LeBron James's mentor is?

A. Magic Johnson
B. Michael Jordan
C. Kobe Bryant
D. Phil

145. LeBron James has how many siblings?

A. One
B. Two
C. Three
D. None

146. LeBron James was born on what day of the week?

A. Monday
B. Friday
C. Saturday
D. Sunday

147. LeBron James's favorite sport is?

A. Soccer
B. Basketball
C. Football
D. Tennis

148. What is LeBron James last name?

A. James
B. Anstin
C. Kim
D. Phil

149. LeBron bridges eras with?

A. Connection
B. Conflict
C. Distance
D. Silence

150. LeBron James was born in which state?

A. Texas
B. Ohio
C. Florida
D. California

151. LeBron friendships are?

A. Short term
B. Transactional
C. Long lasting
D. Random

152. LeBron James's childhood coach was?

A. Phil Jackson
B. Pat Riley
C. Doc Rivers
D. Frank Walker

153. LeBron James won titles with which teams?

A. Heat
B. Lakers
C. Spurs
D. Cavs

154. Youth challenges built his?

A. Fear
B. Resilience
C. Silence
D. Confusion

155. Fans celebrate?

A. His career
B. His acting
C. His cooking
D. His music

156. LeBron James's first gold medal was in?

A. 2004
B. 2008
C. 2012
D. 2016

157. LeBron James's style of play is?

A. Slow
B. Methodical
C. Fast
D. Aggressive

158. LeBron James is seen as?

A. Cheerful
B. Bold
C. Mysterious
D. Innovative

159. LeBron James prefers?

A. Coffee
B. Tea
C. Juice
D. Water

160. LeBron James's best friend is?

A. Chris Paul
B. Kobe Bryant
C. Dwyane Wade
D. Phil

161. LeBron James's closest friend is?

A. Chris Paul
B. Carmelo Anthony
C. Dwyane Wade
D. Phil

162. LeBron James enjoyed which hobby?

A. Dancing
B. Singing
C. Fishing
D. Reading

163. LeBron James was named Rookie of the Year in?

A. 2002
B. 2003
C. 2004
D. 2005

164. LeBron James's highest scoring game was?

A. 50
B. 60
C. 61
D. 62

165. LeBron James's style is?

A. Unique
B. Loud
C. Bold
D. Subtle

166. LeBron James's favorite childhood movie?

A. Space Jam
B. The Lion King
C. Aladdin
D. Pocahontas

167. LeBron James's defense is?

A. Weak
B. Strong
C. Average
D. Good

168. Career records reflect?

A. Short peak
B. Durability
C. Decline
D. Retreat

169. LeBron James is often seen as?

A. Cheerful
B. Realistic
C. Optimistic
D. Dominant

170. LeBron James's favorite band is?

A. Nirvana
B. The Beatles
C. U2
D. Phil

171. Analysts highlight his?

A. Weakness
B. Vision
C. Confusion
D. Errors

172. Growing up influenced his?

A. Leadership
B. Shyness
C. Silence
D. Distance

173. LeBron James's mother is?

A. Vanessa
B. Gloria
C. Maria
D. Savannah

174. LeBron James had a rivalry with?

A. Dwyane Wade
B. Carmelo Anthony
C. Kobe Bryant
D. Phil

175. LeBron James is known to be?

A. Confident
B. Shy
C. Loud
D. Reserved

176. LeBron James's parents worked in?

A. Law
B. Medicine
C. Entertainment
D. Various jobs

177. LeBron James's first career triple-double was in?

A. 2004
B. 2005
C. 2006
D. 2007

178. LeBron James's impact is?

A. Small
B. Medium
C. Huge
D. Moderate

179. LeBron adjusted his?

A. Diet
B. Game style
C. Accent
D. Nickname

180. LeBron James was born on?

A. December 20
B. January 15
C. February 18
D. December 30

181. Fans describe LeBron as?

A. Lazy
B. Ordinary
C. Inspirational
D. Quiet

182. LeBron James is recognized for his?

A. Presence
B. Mystery
C. Strength
D. Leadership

183. LeBron supports his?

A. Brand
B. Rivals
C. Children
D. Critics

184. LeBron James won his first NBA title in?

A. 2010
B. 2011
C. 2012
D. 2013

185. LeBron James is known to avoid?

A. Parties
B. Publicity
C. Social Media
D. Interviews

186. LeBron James's first NBA team was?

A. Lakers
B. Cavs
C. Heat
D. Spurs

187. LeBron James's first pet was a?

A. Dog
B. Cat
C. Fish
D. Hamster

188. LeBron James shares his birthday with?

A. Tiger Woods
B. Kobe Bryant
C. Michael Jordan
D. Phil

189. LeBron is admired for?

A. Acting
B. Writing
C. Leadership
D. Dancing

190. LeBron James's work ethic is?

A. Relaxed
B. Ambitious
C. Strong
D. Driven

191. LeBron James was close to?

A. Kobe Bryant
B. Carmelo Anthony
C. Michael Jordan
D. Phil

192. LeBron James had a conflict with?

A. Kobe Bryant
B. Paul Pierce
C. Carmelo Anthony
D. Phil

193. LeBron learned teamwork from?

A. Isolation
B. Coaches
C. Media
D. Fans

194. LeBron James loves?

A. Cooking
B. Singing
C. Writing
D. Reading

195. Post 2023 LeBron focused on?

A. Decline
B. Legacy
C. Retreat
D. Absence

196. LeBron James's daughter is named?

A. Zuri
B. Bronny
C. Bryce
D. Savannah

197. LeBron James's best friend is?

A. Carmelo Anthony
B. Dwyane Wade
C. Chris Paul
D. Dru Joyce

198. LeBron James became the face of?

A. Adidas
B. Nike
C. Puma
D. Reebok

199. LeBron James is passionate about?

A. Music
B. Reading
C. Art
D. Video games

200. LeBron rise continued through?

A. Decline
B. Injury
C. Adaptation
D. Retirement

201. LeBron media projects show?

A. Storytelling
B. Noise
C. Chaos
D. Silence

202. LeBron rise driven by?

A. Luck
B. Work ethic
C. Timing
D. Hype

203. LeBron James's first Finals appearance was in?

A. 2005
B. 2006
C. 2007
D. 2008

204. LeBron honors his?

A. Coaches
B. Roots
C. Silence
D. Rivals

205. LeBron James was born in which decade?

A. 1970s

B. 1980s

C. 1990s

D. 2000s

206. LeBron James won back-to-back titles in?

A. 2011-2012

B. 2012-2013

C. 2013-2014

D. 2014-2015

207. LeBron James's wife's name is?

A. Savannah

B. Gloria

C. Vanessa

D. Sasha

208. LeBron James's first job was?

A. Waiter

B. Barista

C. Salesman

D. Basketball player

209. LeBron James's mentor is?

A. Michael Jordan
B. Magic Johnson
C. Kobe Bryant
D. Phil

210. LeBron balanced sports with?

A. Neglect
B. School
C. Fame
D. Travel

211. Career rise reflects?

A. Short peak
B. Consistency
C. Collapse
D. Delay

212. LeBron James is known for his?

A. Humor
B. Style
C. Versatility
D. Bravery

213. LeBron James grew up in?

A. Los Angeles
B. New York
C. Miami
D. Akron

214. LeBron is often called?

A. Inconsistent
B. Average
C. Legend
D. Unknown

215. LeBron James was born in the month of?

A. January
B. February
C. December
D. March

216. LeBron James has been praised for his?

A. Humor
B. Commitment
C. Authenticity
D. Work ethic

217. LeBron James's birth year is?

A. 1982
B. 1983
C. 1984
D. 1985

218. LeBron James's son is named?

A. Bryce
B. LeBron Jr.
C. Xavier
D. Phil

219. LeBron James joined the Lakers in?

A. 2016
B. 2017
C. 2018
D. 2019

220. LeBron balances fame with?

A. Distance
B. Control
C. Family time
D. Secrecy

221. Early mentors guided his?

A. Career
B. Accent
C. Hobbies
D. Style

222. His upbringing shaped his?

A. Attitude
B. Voice
C. Clothes
D. Accent

223. LeBron James's first MVP was in?

A. 2007
B. 2008
C. 2009
D. 2010

224. He inspires?

A. Young athletes
B. Politicians
C. Doctors
D. Teachers

225. Critics praise LeBron James's?

A. Speed
B. Strength
C. IQ
D. Shooting

226. LeBron background shaped his?

A. Style
B. Accent
C. Character
D. Nickname

227. LeBron James is famous for?

A. Acting
B. Singing
C. Basketball
D. Modeling

228. LeBron James's close friend is?

A. Kobe Bryant
B. Michael Jordan
C. Dwyane Wade
D. Carmelo Anthony

229. LeBron James has been married since?

A. 2009
B. 2010
C. 2012
D. 2013

230. LeBron James's first major contract was with?

A. Nike
B. Adidas
C. Puma
D. Reebok

231. LeBron James is allergic to?

A. Peanuts
B. Cats
C. Dogs
D. Gluten

232. LeBron James joined the Lakers in?

A. 2016
B. 2017
C. 2018
D. 2019

233. LeBron James's close friend is?

A. Chris Paul
B. Kobe Bryant
C. Dwyane Wade
D. Phil

234. LeBron achievements span?

A. Few years
B. Many eras
C. One team
D. College

235. LeBron James played for which college?

A. None
B. Duke
C. UCLA
D. UNC

236. LeBron James won his 4th title in?

A. 2018
B. 2019
C. 2020
D. 2021

237. LeBron James is considered?

A. Confident
B. Quirky
C. Versatile
D. Dominant

238. LeBron James's first coach was?

A. Phil Jackson
B. Pat Riley
C. Doc Rivers
D. Paul Silas

239. LeBron James is appreciated for his?

A. Humility
B. Wealth
C. Authenticity
D. Leadership

240. LeBron James's zodiac sign is?

A. Pisces
B. Taurus
C. Leo
D. Capricorn

241. LeBron James's presence on court is?

A. Subtle
B. Commanding
C. Quiet
D. Soft

242. Teammates respect his?

A. Ego
B. Leadership
C. Distance
D. Silence

243. LeBron is seen as?

A. Rookie
B. Veteran
C. Coach
D. Manager

244. LeBron James's birthstone is?

A. Ruby
B. Diamond
C. Emerald
D. Garnet

245. Fans admire his?

A. Leadership
B. Shyness
C. Silence
D. Laziness

246. LeBron spouse is?

A. Kim
B. Kelly
C. Savannah
D. Rihanna

247. LeBron family appears in?

A. Rumors
B. Media moments
C. Conflicts
D. Scandals

248. LeBron invests in?

A. Sports teams
B. Food trucks
C. Farms
D. Casinos

249. LeBron James is primarily known as a?

A. Guard
B. Forward
C. Center
D. Coach

250. Where was LeBron James born?

A. Texas
B. Florida
C. California
D. Ohio

251. LeBron James has a strong bond with?

A. Chris Paul
B. Kobe Bryant
C. Dwyane Wade
D. Phil

252. LeBron friendships built on?

A. Trust
B. Drama
C. Conflict
D. Distance

253. LeBron James joined the Lakers in?

A. 2016
B. 2017
C. 2018
D. 2019

254. His leadership evolved with?

A. Age
B. Silence
C. Distance
D. Conflict

255. LeBron birth year places him?

A. Teen
B. Young adult
C. Veteran
D. Retired

256. LeBron praises?

A. Opponents
B. Silence
C. Errors
D. Failures

257. LeBron James is a fan of?

A. Romance
B. Horror
C. Comedies
D. Action

258. LeBron James's height is?

A. 6'4"
B. 6'6"
C. 6'8"
D. 7'0"

259. LeBron James's personality is?

A. Charismatic
B. Loud
C. Outgoing
D. Reserved

260. LeBron James's childhood friend was?

A. Dwyane Wade
B. Carmelo Anthony
C. Chris Paul
D. Dru Joyce

261. LeBron James dreamed of becoming a?

A. Doctor

B. Lawyer

C. Veterinarian

D. Basketball player

262. Legends praise LeBron legacy?

A. Brief

B. Limited

C. Historic

D. Average

263. Historic moment includes?

A. Retirement

B. Record scoring

C. Coaching

D. Decline

264. LeBron James's nickname is?

A. Magic

B. King James

C. Big Shot

D. Bron

265. LeBron James is fluent in?

A. French
B. Spanish
C. English
D. German

266. LeBron James won his 4th MVP in?

A. 2010
B. 2011
C. 2012
D. 2013

267. LeBron James was rumored to date?

A. Rihanna
B. Kim Kardashian
C. BeyoncÃ©
D. Jennifer Lopez

268. LeBron James loved which food as a child?

A. Pizza
B. Pasta
C. Burgers
D. Fried chicken

269. LeBron James was once in a relationship with?

A. Rihanna
B. BeyoncÃ©
C. Kim Kardashian
D. Kate Hudson

270. LeBron James's court vision is?

A. Average
B. Exceptional
C. Poor
D. Good

271. LeBron early life inspires?

A. Critics
B. Youth
C. Rivals
D. Haters

272. LeBron James's presence is?

A. Soft
B. Strong
C. Subtle
D. Commanding

273. LeBron James is known for his?

A. Shooting
B. Dunking
C. Defense
D. Passing

274. Opponents credit LeBron for?

A. Fear
B. Tactics
C. Experience
D. Noise

275. LeBron James's first sport was?

A. Soccer
B. Basketball
C. Football
D. Baseball

276. LeBron James is often?

A. Calm
B. Mysterious
C. Cheerful
D. Innovative

277. LeBron James is seen as?

A. Mysterious
B. Innovative
C. Quirky
D. Bold

278. LeBron influences?

A. Sports
B. Tech
C. Politics
D. Cooking

279. LeBron James's first pet was a?

A. Dog
B. Cat
C. Bird
D. Hamster

280. LeBron James's first MVP award was in?

A. 2007
B. 2008
C. 2009
D. 2010

281. LeBron James's basketball IQ is?

A. Average

B. Low

C. High

D. Exceptional

282. LeBron James collaborated with?

A. Chris Paul

B. Dwyane Wade

C. Kobe Bryant

D. Phil

283. Birth city is often mentioned?

A. Rarely

B. Never

C. Sometimes

D. Often

284. LeBron James's astrological sign is?

A. Aries

B. Gemini

C. Leo

D. Capricorn

285. LeBron youth focused on?

A. Music
B. Travel
C. Sports
D. Art

286. LeBron James's co-star was?

A. Anthony Davis
B. Chris Paul
C. Kobe Bryant
D. Phil

287. His image is?

A. Bold
B. Quiet
C. Shy
D. Ordinary

288. LeBron achieved longevity through?

A. Luck
B. Training
C. Chance
D. Silence

289. LeBron James married?

A. Savannah Brinson
B. Gabrielle Union
C. Kim Kardashian
D. Phil

290. LeBron rise shows?

A. Stagnation
B. Growth
C. Confusion
D. Loss

291. Public views LeBron as?

A. Divider
B. Unclear
C. Leader
D. Unknown

292. LeBron James's first team was?

A. Cavs
B. Lakers
C. Heat
D. Spurs

293. LeBron James has how many children?

A. 2
B. 3
C. 4
D. 5

294. LeBron nickname is?

A. Flash
B. Chef
C. King James
D. Agent

295. LeBron James is known as?

A. Coach
B. Actor
C. Singer
D. Athlete

296. LeBron values?

A. Privacy
B. Fame
C. Family
D. Distance

297. Competitive spirit drives?

A. Rivalries
B. Silence
C. Retreat
D. Avoidance

298. LeBron birthday month?

A. June
B. March
C. December
D. April

299. LeBron James is admired for his?

A. Bravery
B. Humor
C. Intelligence
D. Leadership

300. LeBron James attended which high school?

A. St. Vincent-St. Mary
B. Laurel Springs
C. Harvard-Westlake
D. Phil

1. LeBron James wears which jersey number?

23

2. Critics admire his?

Longevity

3. LeBron James's demeanor is?

Confident

4. LeBron active online via?

Posts

5. LeBron James was a fan of?

Football

6. LeBron James grew up watching which sport?

Football

7. LeBron story starts in?

Small town

8. LeBron James played which position in football?

Receiver

9. NBA peers see LeBron as?

Leader

10. His hometown fame grew due to?

Sports

11. LeBron James's birth city is?

Akron

12. LeBron James's ex-teammate is?

Dwyane Wade

13. LeBron James's first child is?

Bronny

14. LeBron James's rival is?

Carmelo Anthony

15. LeBron James has won how many MVP awards?

4

16. LeBron James's first Finals MVP was in?

2012

17. LeBron James's brother's name is?

He has none

18. LeBron James's first NBA title was with?

Heat

19. LeBron was born in?

Akron

20. LeBron James loves?

Pizza

21. Early talent was?

Exceptional

22. LeBron James is appreciated for his?

Versatility

23. LeBron James has a fear of?

Heights

24. LeBron is also a?

Producer

25. LeBron James won back-to-back titles in?

2012-2013

26. LeBron James's favorite holiday is?

Christmas

27. LeBron James had a public relationship with?

Savannah Brinson

28. LeBron James's favorite movie is?

Space Jam

29. LeBron James rose to fame with?

Cavs

30. LeBron James is described as?

Bold

31. LeBron marriage known for?

Stability

32. LeBron James is known for his?

Work ethic

33. LeBron James's favorite color is?

Black

34. LeBron plays mainly as?

Forward

35. LeBron James was drafted by?

Cavs

36. LeBron James is respected for his?

Work ethic

37. LeBron James became the all-time leading scorer in?

2023

38. LeBron James starred in which movie?

Space Jam

39. LeBron James's presence is?

Commanding

40. LeBron James's middle name is?

Ramon

41. LeBron James was named Athlete of the Year by?

Sports Illustrated

42. LeBron James's NBA debut was in?

2003

43. LeBron James learned to read at age?

5

44. LeBron James has a tattoo of?

A Crown

45. LeBron James was born under which Chinese zodiac?

Rat

46. LeBron is praised for?

Skill

47. LeBron James led the league in scoring in?

2008

48. League respect comes from?

Legacy

49. LeBron James was raised in which city?

Akron

50. LeBron James's middle name is?

Ramon

51. LeBron James's playing style is?

Aggressive

52. Commentators note his?

Basketball IQ

53. LeBron James's persona is?

Commanding

54. LeBron career spans?

Two decades

55. LeBron James's highest scoring game was?

61

56. LeBron James is often described as?

Dominant

57. LeBron childhood taught?

Discipline

58. LeBron interests include?

Wine collecting

59. LeBron James was born during which year?

1984

60. LeBron teammates value his?

Leadership

61. LeBron James won his first title in?

2012

62. LeBron James is admired for his?

Commitment

63. LeBron respects his?

Roots

64. LeBron James's mother encouraged him to?

Play sports

65. LeBron James was born in which hospital?

Summa

66. LeBron James's favorite book is?

Harry Potter

67. LeBron James is friends with?

Chris Paul

68. LeBron James's birth state is?

Ohio

69. LeBron James's persona is?

Outspoken

70. LeBron James won his first MVP in?

2009

71. LeBron James's first dunk was at age?

14

72. LeBron James's performances are?

Aggressive

73. LeBron James was drafted by?

Cavs

74. LeBron mentors?

Young players

75. LeBron is seen as?

Legend

76. LeBron adapted to?

New roles

77. Media praise LeBron for?

Durability

78. LeBron known for?

Discipline

79. LeBron impact remained?

Strong

80. LeBron James grew up in which neighborhood?

Spring Hill

81. Fun side shows his?

Human side

82. LeBron milestone includes?

Father son duo

83. LeBron James's presence is often?

Calm

84. Fans admire LeBron James's?

Work ethic

85. Legacy milestones highlight?

Impact

86. LeBron James's longest friendship is with?

Dru Joyce

87. Veteran role expanded his?

Mentorship

88. LeBron James's favorite actor is?

Denzel Washington

89. People view him as?

Trailblazer

90. LeBron James had a rivalry with?

Paul Pierce

91. LeBron James won his first NBA title in?

2012

92. LeBron James was drafted in which year?

2003

93. Personal life reflects?

Focus

94. LeBron James's first coach was?

Frank Walker

95. LeBron James's first team was?

Cavs

96. LeBron James's influence is?

Global

97. LeBron crossed which scoring mark?

40000

98. LeBron James was drafted by?

Cavs

99. LeBron James's first MVP was in?

2009

100. LeBron milestone seasons show?

Stability

101. LeBron James's childhood nickname was?

Bron

102. LeBron James is seen as a?

Leader

103. LeBron James played with?

Dwyane Wade

104. He is famous for?

Basketball

105. LeBron James led the league in assists in?

2020

106. LeBron James is close friends with?

Dwyane Wade

107. LeBron James's first name is?

LeBron

108. LeBron James was named All-Star MVP in?

2006

109. LeBron James is also known as?

The King

110. LeBron fitness routine is?

Strict

111. Which team is linked to LeBron in 2025?

Lakers

112. LeBron James is described as?

Versatile

113. LeBron birthplace state?

Ohio

114. LeBron James's first car was a?

Hummer

115. LeBron enjoys?

Training

116. LeBron rivals respect his?

Experience

117. LeBron James's favorite player growing up?

Michael Jordan

118. LeBron avoids public?

Feuds

119. LeBron legacy feels?

Lasting

120. LeBron James's first Finals MVP was in?

2012

121. LeBron James's first All-Star MVP was in?

2006

122. What is LeBron James last name?

James

123. LeBron James's current partner is?

Savannah Brinson

124. LeBron James's favorite subject was?

English

125. LeBron business ventures include?

Media

126. LeBron James was born in which city?

Akron

127. LeBron James was supported by?

Dwyane Wade

128. LeBron James was born during which season?

Winter

129. Career highs continued with?

Adaptation

130. LeBron James's favorite food is?

Pizza

131. LeBron roots connect to?

Akron

132. LeBron James is seen as?

Innovative

133. LeBron James's ex-teammate is?

Dwyane Wade

134. Family life keeps him?

Grounded

135. LeBron James's first scoring title was in?

2008

136. LeBron off court passion?

Youth programs

137. LeBron James's breakout year was?

2003

138. LeBron James's first All-Star game was in?

2005

139. Which sport defines LeBron?

Basketball

140. LeBron James has worked with?

Dwyane Wade

141. LeBron James was criticized by?

Paul Pierce

142. LeBron James became the face of which brand?

Nike

143. All time status earned by?

Consistency

144. LeBron James's mentor is?

Magic Johnson

145. LeBron James has how many siblings?

None

146. LeBron James was born on what day of the week?

Saturday

147. LeBron James's favorite sport is?

Football

148. What is LeBron James last name?

James

149. LeBron bridges eras with?

Connection

150. LeBron James was born in which state?

Ohio

151. LeBron friendships are?

Long lasting

152. LeBron James's childhood coach was?

Frank Walker

153. LeBron James won titles with which teams?

Lakers

154. Youth challenges built his?

Resilience

155. Fans celebrate?

His career

156. LeBron James's first gold medal was in?

2008

157. LeBron James's style of play is?

Aggressive

158. LeBron James is seen as?

Innovative

159. LeBron James prefers?

Water

160. LeBron James's best friend is?

Dwyane Wade

161. LeBron James's closest friend is?

Dwyane Wade

162. LeBron James enjoyed which hobby?

Reading

163. LeBron James was named Rookie of the Year in?

2004

164. LeBron James's highest scoring game was?

61

165. LeBron James's style is?

Bold

166. LeBron James's favorite childhood movie?

Space Jam

167. LeBron James's defense is?

Strong

168. Career records reflect?

Durability

169. LeBron James is often seen as?

Dominant

170. LeBron James's favorite band is?

U2

171. Analysts highlight his?

Vision

172. Growing up influenced his?

Leadership

173. LeBron James's mother is?

Gloria

174. LeBron James had a rivalry with?

Kobe Bryant

175. LeBron James is known to be?

Confident

176. LeBron James's parents worked in?

Various jobs

177. LeBron James's first career triple-double was in?

2005

178. LeBron James's impact is?

Huge

179. LeBron adjusted his?

Game style

180. LeBron James was born on?

December 30

181. Fans describe LeBron as?

Inspirational

182. LeBron James is recognized for his?

Leadership

183. LeBron supports his?

Children

184. LeBron James won his first NBA title in?

2012

185. LeBron James is known to avoid?

Social Media

186. LeBron James's first NBA team was?

Cavs

187. LeBron James's first pet was a?

Dog

188. LeBron James shares his birthday with?

Tiger Woods

189. LeBron is admired for?

Leadership

190. LeBron James's work ethic is?

Driven

191. LeBron James was close to?

Kobe Bryant

192. LeBron James had a conflict with?

Paul Pierce

193. LeBron learned teamwork from?

Coaches

194. LeBron James loves?

Reading

195. Post 2023 LeBron focused on?

Legacy

196. LeBron James's daughter is named?

Zuri

197. LeBron James's best friend is?

Dru Joyce

198. LeBron James became the face of?

Nike

199. LeBron James is passionate about?

Video games

200. LeBron rise continued through?

Adaptation

201. LeBron media projects show?

Storytelling

202. LeBron rise driven by?

Work ethic

203. LeBron James's first Finals appearance was in?

2007

204. LeBron honors his?

Roots

205. LeBron James was born in which decade?

1980s

206. LeBron James won back-to-back titles in?

2012-2013

207. LeBron James's wife's name is?

Savannah

208. LeBron James's first job was?

Basketball player

209. LeBron James's mentor is?

Magic Johnson

210. LeBron balanced sports with?

School

211. Career rise reflects?

Consistency

212. LeBron James is known for his?

Versatility

213. LeBron James grew up in?

Akron

214. LeBron is often called?

Legend

215. LeBron James was born in the month of?

December

216. LeBron James has been praised for his?

Work ethic

217. LeBron James's birth year is?

1984

218. LeBron James's son is named?

LeBron Jr.

219. LeBron James joined the Lakers in?

2018

220. LeBron balances fame with?

Family time

221. Early mentors guided his?

Career

222. His upbringing shaped his?

Attitude

223. LeBron James's first MVP was in?

2009

224. He inspires?

Young athletes

225. Critics praise LeBron James's?

IQ

226. LeBron background shaped his?

Character

227. LeBron James is famous for?

Basketball

228. LeBron James's close friend is?

Dwyane Wade

229. LeBron James has been married since?

2013

230. LeBron James's first major contract was with?

Nike

231. LeBron James is allergic to?

Gluten

232. LeBron James joined the Lakers in?

2018

233. LeBron James's close friend is?

Chris Paul

234. LeBron achievements span?

Many eras

235. LeBron James played for which college?

None

236. LeBron James won his 4th title in?

2020

237. LeBron James is considered?

Dominant

238. LeBron James's first coach was?

Paul Silas

239. LeBron James is appreciated for his?

Leadership

240. LeBron James's zodiac sign is?

Capricorn

241. LeBron James's presence on court is?

Commanding

242. Teammates respect his?

Leadership

243. LeBron is seen as?

Veteran

244. LeBron James's birthstone is?

Garnet

245. Fans admire his?

Leadership

246. LeBron spouse is?

Savannah

247. LeBron family appears in?

Media moments

248. LeBron invests in?

Sports teams

249. LeBron James is primarily known as a?

Forward

250. Where was LeBron James born?

Ohio

251. LeBron James has a strong bond with?

Dwyane Wade

252. LeBron friendships built on?

Trust

253. LeBron James joined the Lakers in?

2018

254. His leadership evolved with?

Age

255. LeBron birth year places him?

Veteran

256. LeBron praises?

Opponents

257. LeBron James is a fan of?

Action

258. LeBron James's height is?

6'8"

259. LeBron James's personality is?

Charismatic

260. LeBron James's childhood friend was?

Dru Joyce

261. LeBron James dreamed of becoming a?

Basketball player

262. Legends praise LeBron legacy?

Historic

263. Historic moment includes?

Record scoring

264. LeBron James's nickname is?

King James

265. LeBron James is fluent in?

English

266. LeBron James won his 4th MVP in?

2013

267. LeBron James was rumored to date?

Rihanna

268. LeBron James loved which food as a child?

Fried chicken

269. LeBron James was once in a relationship with?

Rihanna

270. LeBron James's court vision is?

Exceptional

271. LeBron early life inspires?

Youth

272. LeBron James's presence is?

Commanding

273. LeBron James is known for his?

Passing

274. Opponents credit LeBron for?

Experience

275. LeBron James's first sport was?

Football

276. LeBron James is often?

Innovative

277. LeBron James is seen as?

Innovative

278. LeBron influences?

Sports

279. LeBron James's first pet was a?

Dog

280. LeBron James's first MVP award was in?

2009

281. LeBron James's basketball IQ is?

Exceptional

282. LeBron James collaborated with?

Chris Paul

283. Birth city is often mentioned?

Often

284. LeBron James's astrological sign is?

Capricorn

285. LeBron youth focused on?

Sports

286. LeBron James's co-star was?

Anthony Davis

287. His image is?

Bold

288. LeBron achieved longevity through?

Training

289. LeBron James married?

Savannah Brinson

290. LeBron rise shows?

Growth

291. Public views LeBron as?

Leader

292. LeBron James's first team was?

Cavs

293. LeBron James has how many children?

3

294. LeBron nickname is?

King James

295. LeBron James is known as?

Athlete

296. LeBron values?

Family

297. Competitive spirit drives?

Rivalries

298. LeBron birthday month?

December

299. LeBron James is admired for his?

Leadership

300. LeBron James attended which high school?

St. Vincent-St. Mary

Puzzle 1

ACROSS
1. Anna Paquin
2. Al Pacino
3. Ariana Grande

DOWN
1. Aaron Rodgers
2. Angelina Jolie
3. Anthony Joshua
4. Andrew Lincoln
5. Barack Obama
6. Adam Sandler

Puzzle 2

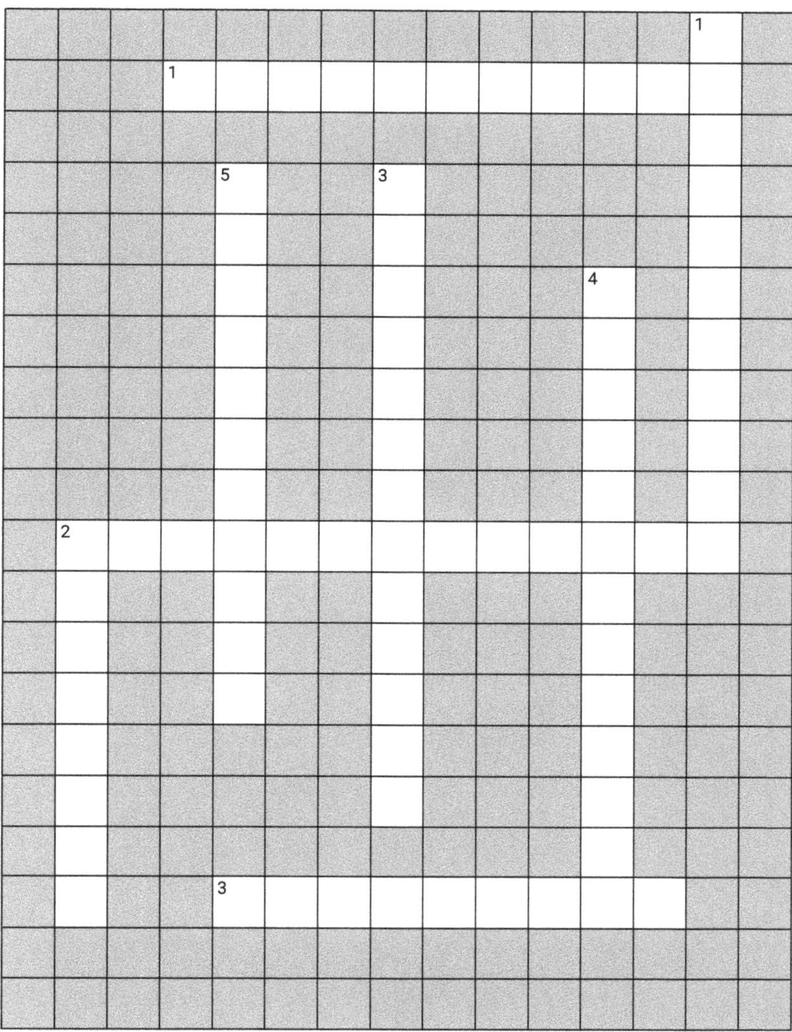

ACROSS
1. Bryce Harper
2. Bernie Sanders
3. Bruno Mars

DOWN
1. Bruce Willis
2. Brad Pitt
3. Britney Spears
4. Bradley Cooper
5. Bill Clinton

Puzzle 3

ACROSS

1. Clint Eastwood

DOWN

1. Charlize Theron
2. Cristiano Ronaldo
3. Dakota Johnson
4. Chris Evans
5. Chris Hemsworth
6. Chris Paul

Puzzle 4

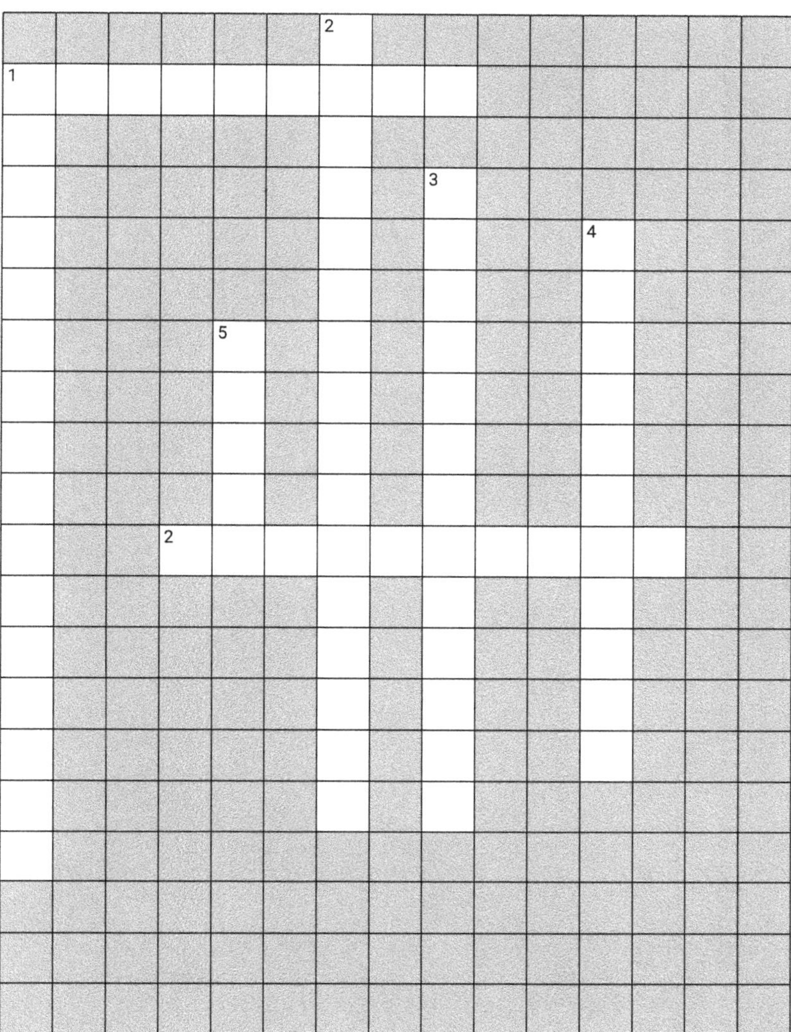

ACROSS
1. Drew Brees
2. Demi Lovato

DOWN
1. David Copperfield
2. Denzel Washington
3. Dwayne Johnson
4. Donald Trump
5. Drake

Puzzle 5

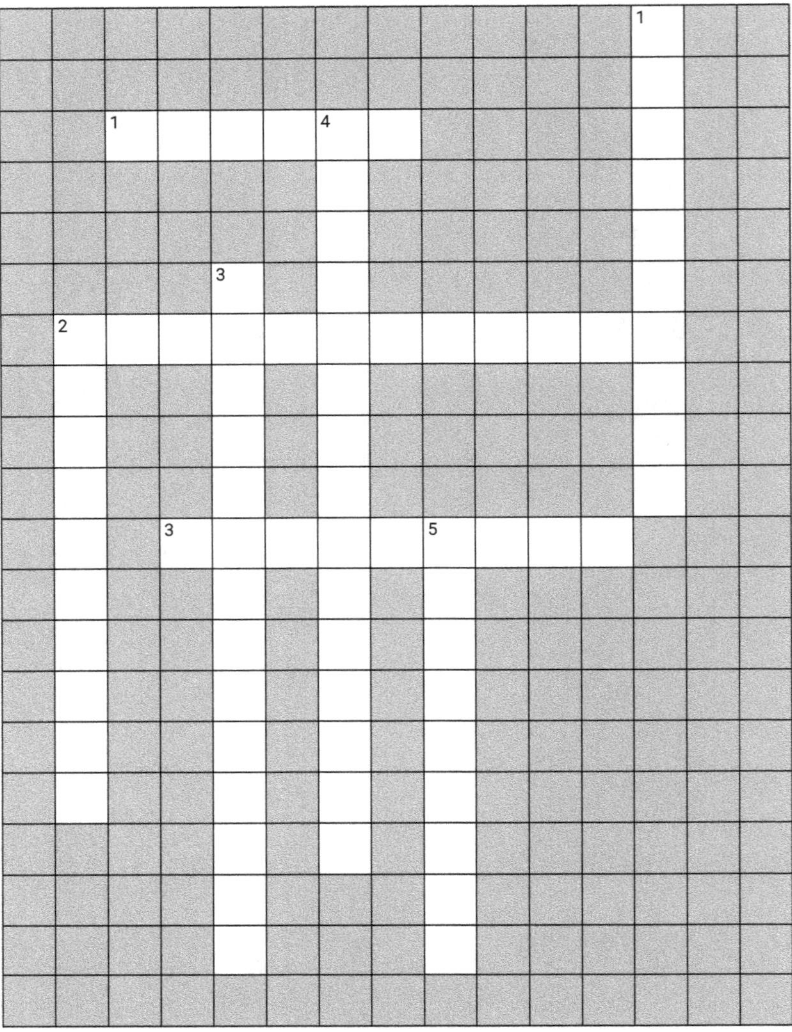

ACROSS
1. Eminem
2. Emilia Clarke
3. Ed Sheeran

DOWN
1. Halle Berry
2. Emma Watson
3. Ellen DeGeneres
4. Elizabeth Warren
5. Elton John

Puzzle 6

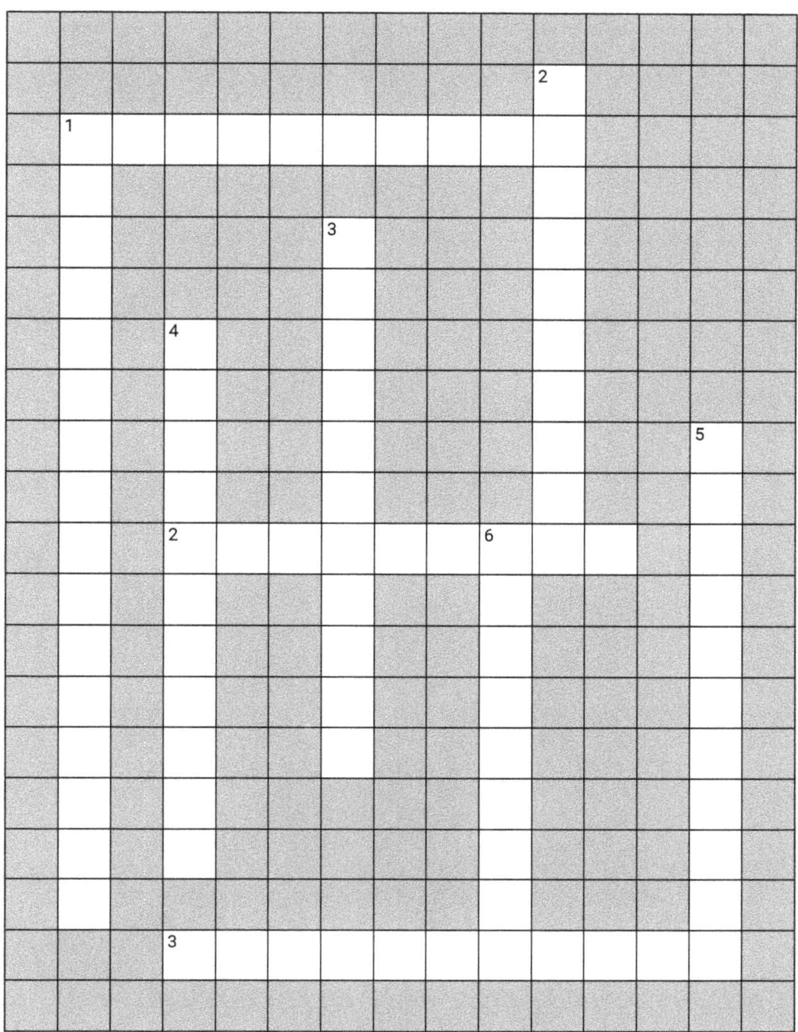

ACROSS
1. Jason Momoa
2. J.K. Rowling
3. James Harden

DOWN
1. Jada Pinkett Smith
2. Jackie Chan
3. Jamie Dornan
4. Hugh Jackman
5. Howard Stern
6. Idris Elba

Puzzle 7

ACROSS
1. Joe Biden
2. Jason Statham

DOWN
1. John Cena
2. Jeffrey Dean Morgan
3. Jennifer Lawrence
4. Jennifer Aniston
5. Jay-Z

Puzzle 8

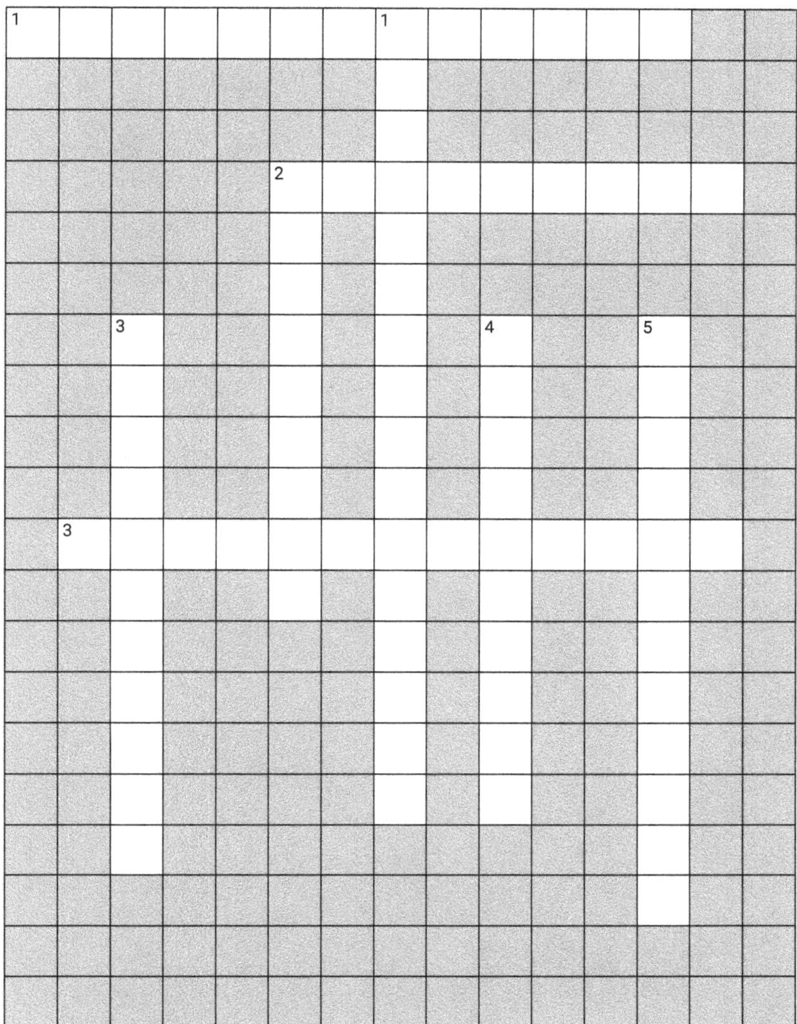

ACROSS
1. Kendall Jenner
2. Katy Perry
3. Judy Sheindlin

DOWN
1. Justin Timberlake
2. Kanye West
3. Keanu Reeves
4. Johnny Depp
5. Justin Bieber

Puzzle 9

ACROSS
1. Kobe Bryant
2. Lady Gaga
3. Kim Kardashian

DOWN
1. Kit Harington
2. Kylie Jenner
3. LeBron James
4. Kourtney Kardashian
5. Khloe Kardashian

Puzzle 10

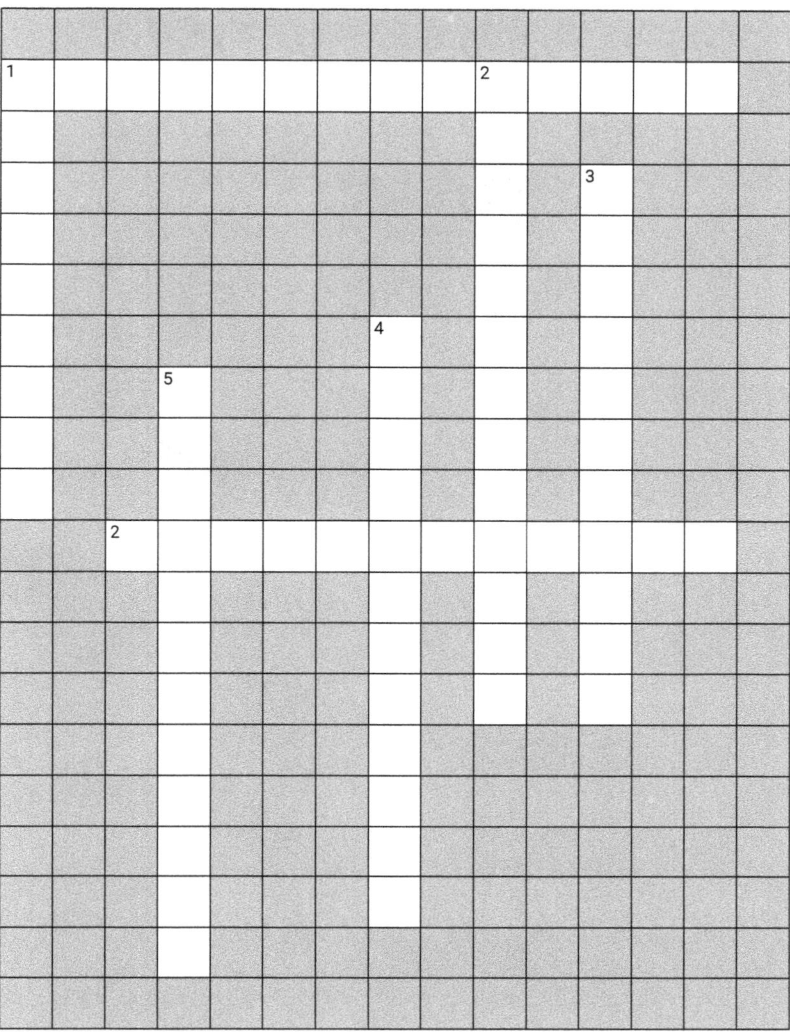

ACROSS
1. Maisie Williams
2. Mark Wahlberg

DOWN
1. Matt Damon
2. Lewis Hamilton
3. Lionel Messi
4. Meghan Markle
5. Melania Trump

Puzzle 11

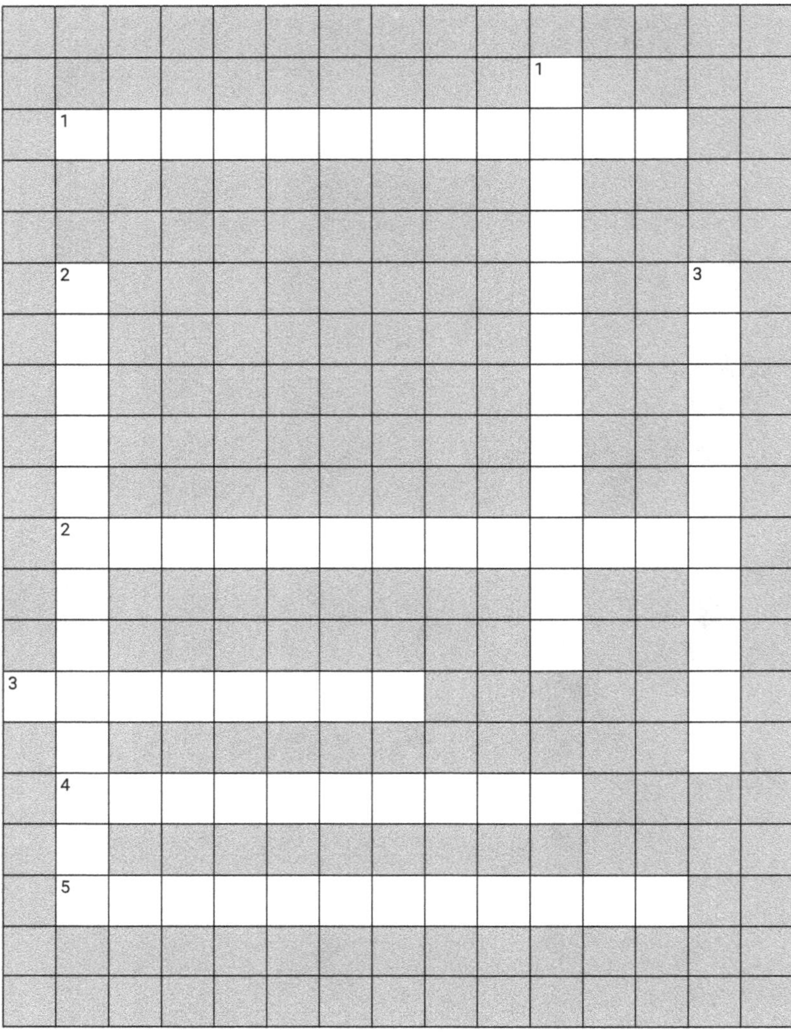

ACROSS
1. Oprah Winfrey
2. Novak Djokovic
3. Neymar Jr
4. Mitt Romney
5. Norman Reedus

DOWN
1. Orlando Bloom
2. Morgan Freeman
3. Miley Cyrus

Puzzle 12

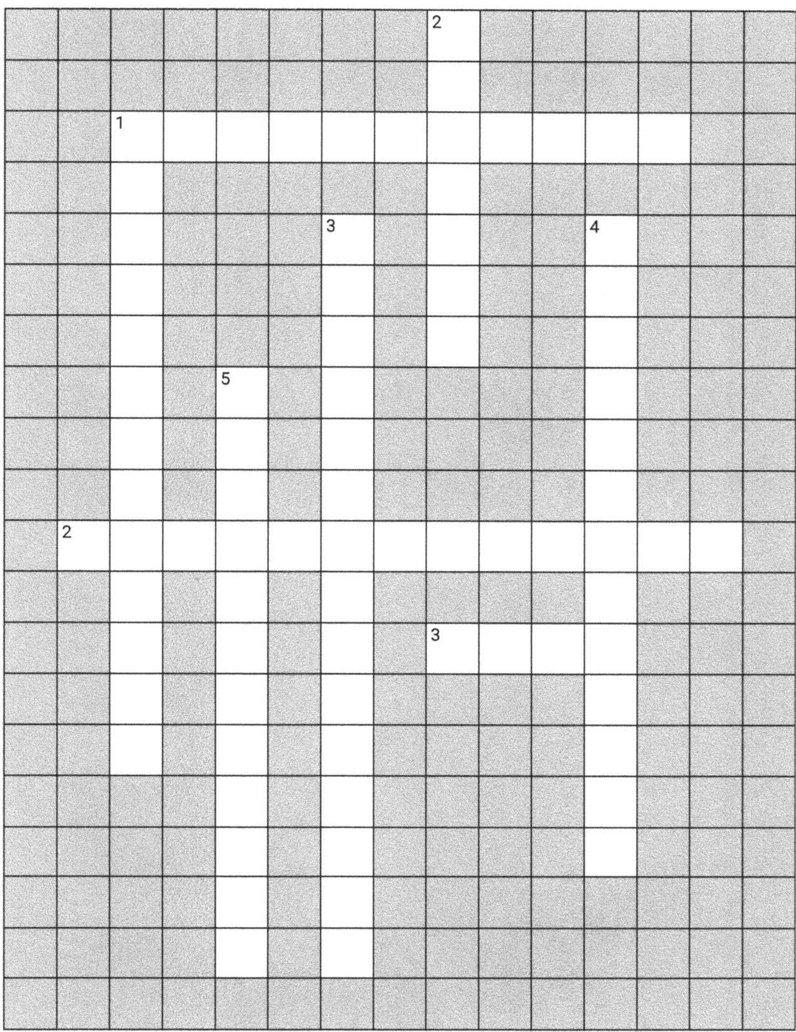

ACROSS
1. Prince Harry
2. Pete Buttigieg
3. Pink

DOWN
1. Phil Mickelson
2. Rihanna
3. Previous Mockups
4. Peter Dinklage
5. Robert De Niro

Puzzle 13

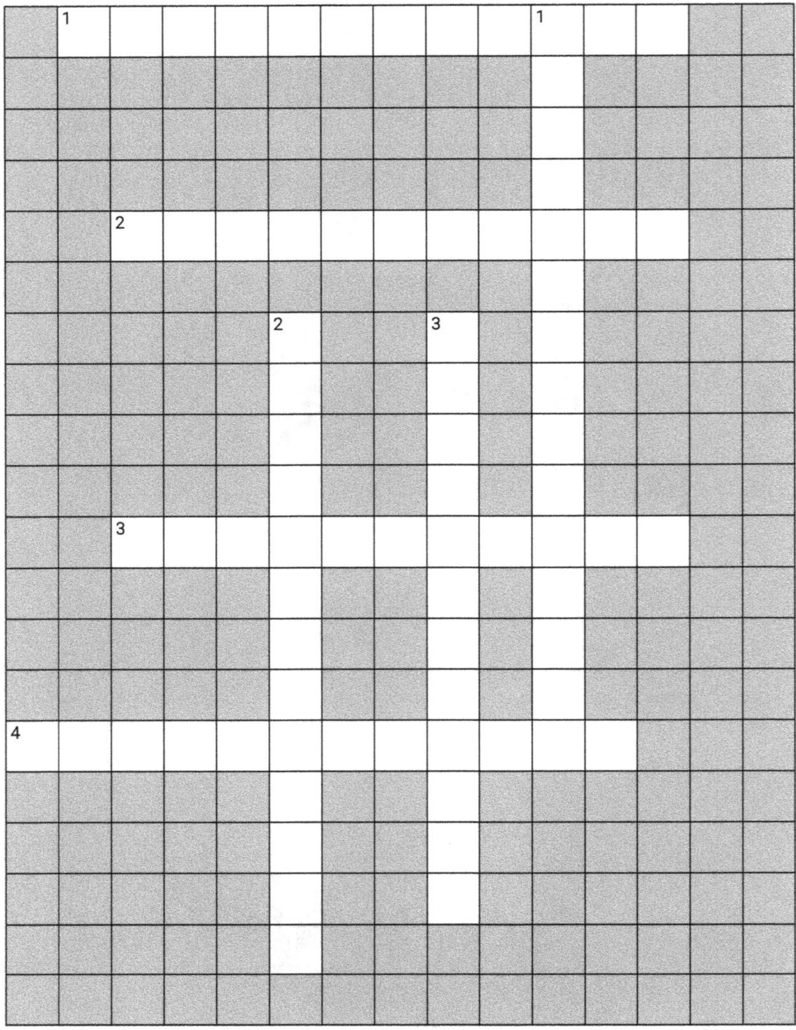

ACROSS
1. Roger Federer
2. Rory McIlroy
3. Ryan Gosling
4. Russell Brand

DOWN
1. Robert Pattinson
2. Robin Williams
3. Ryan Seacrest

Puzzle 14

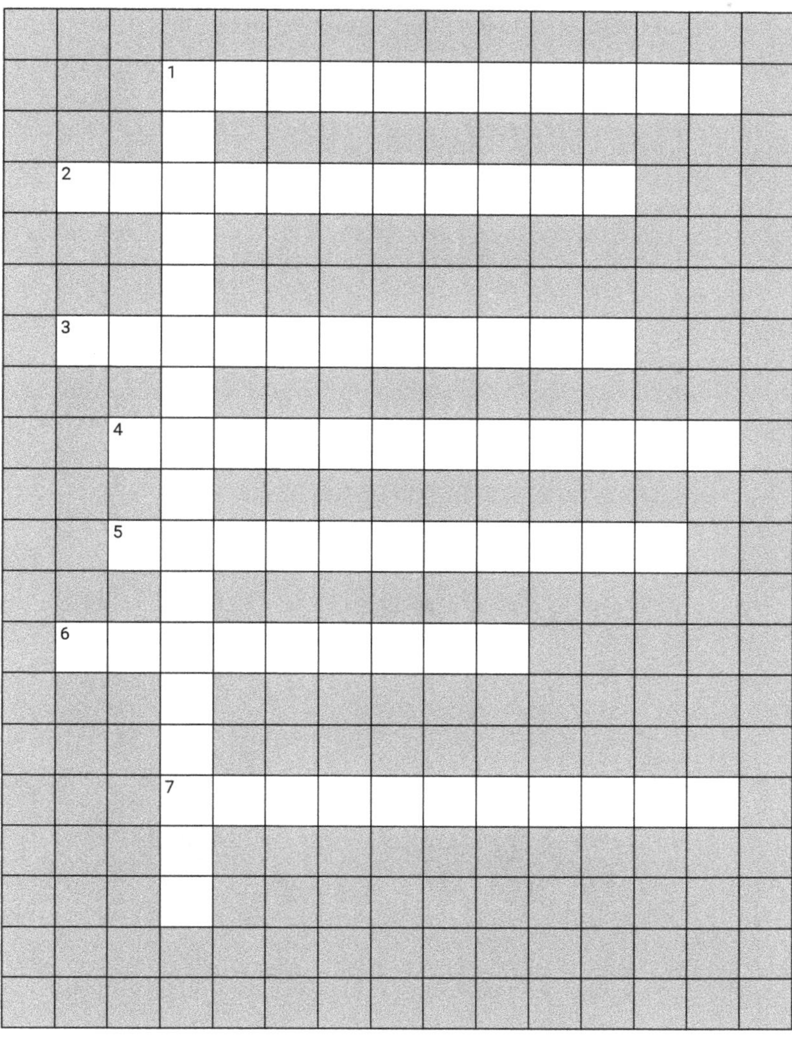

ACROSS
1. Simon Cowell
2. Shawn Mendes
3. Stephen King
4. Stephen Curry
5. Sofía Vergara
6. Sean Combs
7. Selena Gomez

DOWN
1. Scarlett Johansson

Puzzle 15

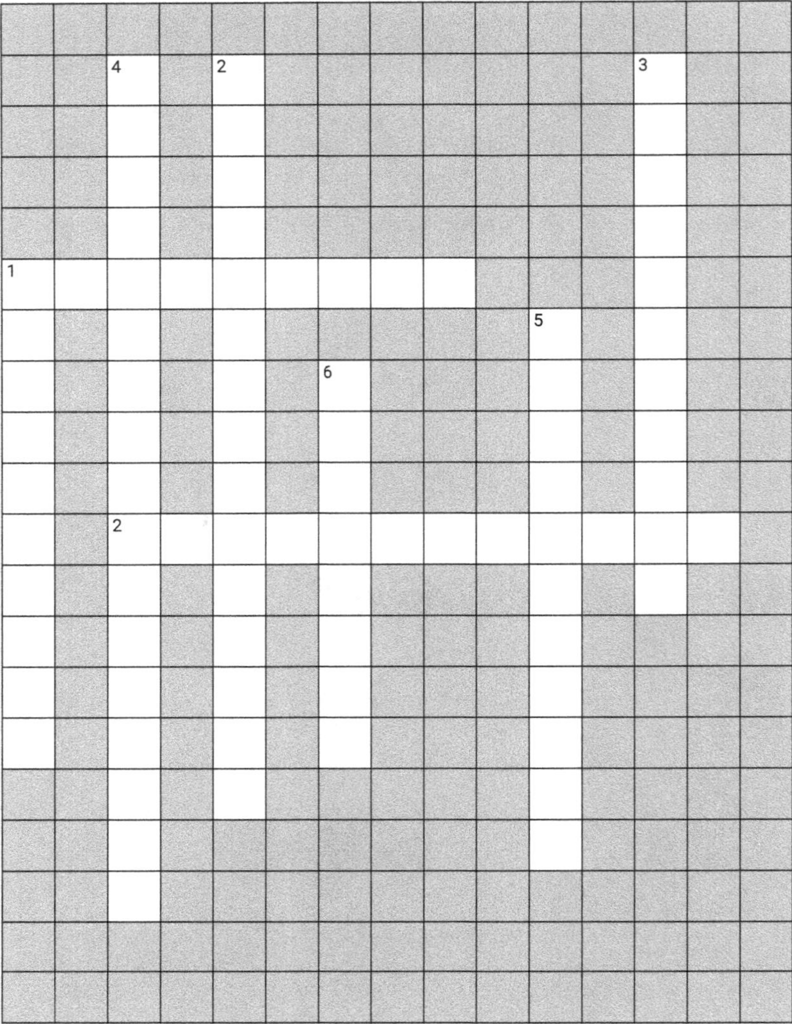

ACROSS
1. The Weeknd
2. Stephen Moyer

DOWN
1. Tiger Woods
2. Steven Spielberg
3. Steve Harvey
4. Sylvester Stallone
5. Taylor Swift
6. Tom Hanks

Puzzle 1

1 ANNAPAQUIN
2 ALPACINO
3 ARIANAGRANDE
1 AARONRODGERS
2 ANGELINAJOLIE
3 ANTHONYJOSHUA
4 ANDREWLINCOLN
5 BARACKOBAMA
6 ADAMSANDLER

Puzzle 2

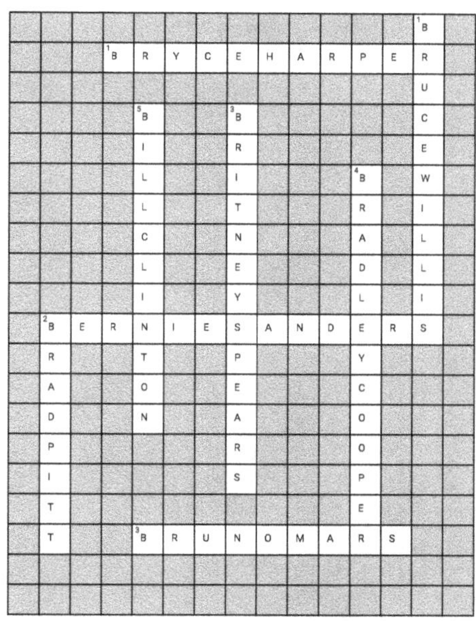

Puzzle 3

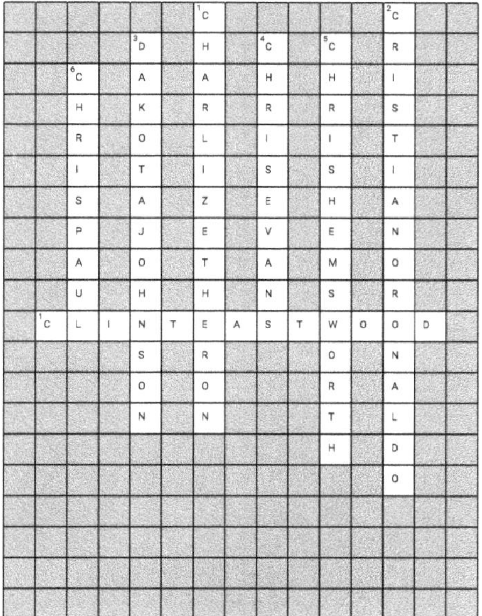

Puzzle 4

1 DREWBREES
2 DEMILOVATO
1 DAVIDCOPPERFIELD
2 DENZELWASHINGTON
3 DWAYNEJOHNSON
4 DONALDTRUMP
5 DRAKE

Puzzle 5

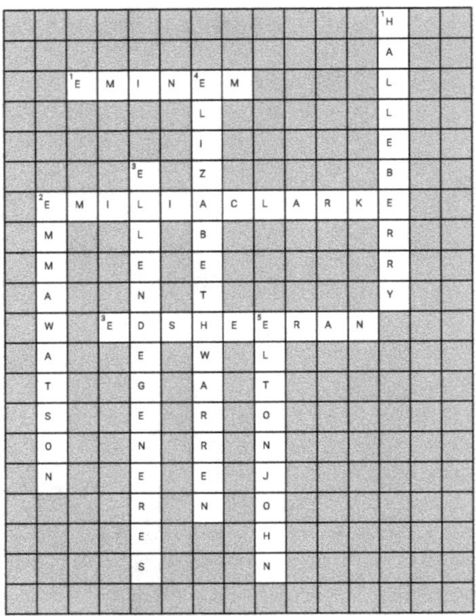

Puzzle 6

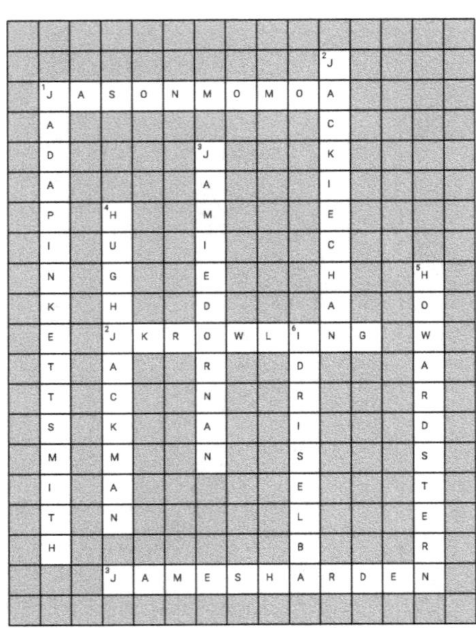

Puzzle 7

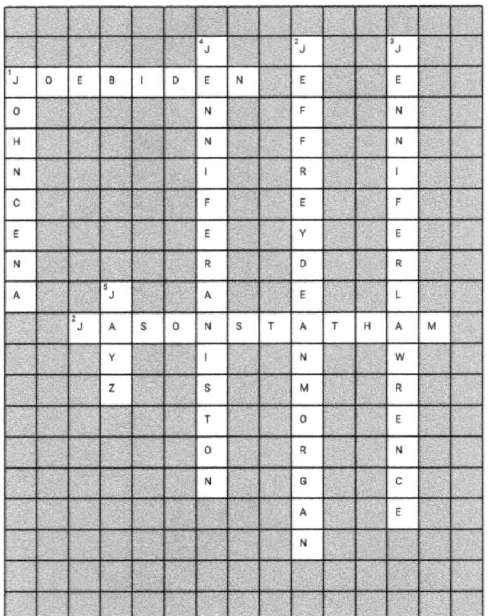

Puzzle 8

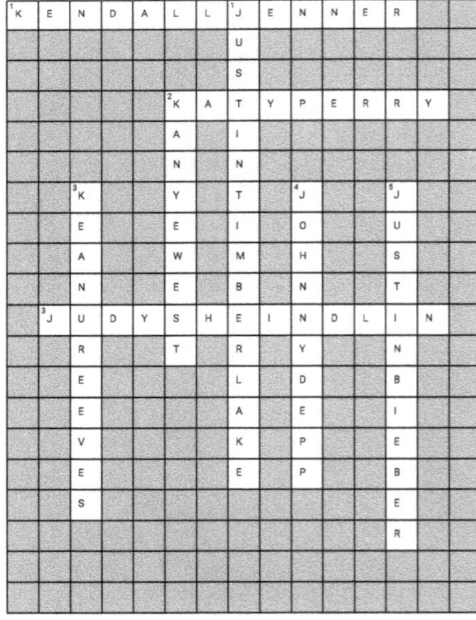

Puzzle 9

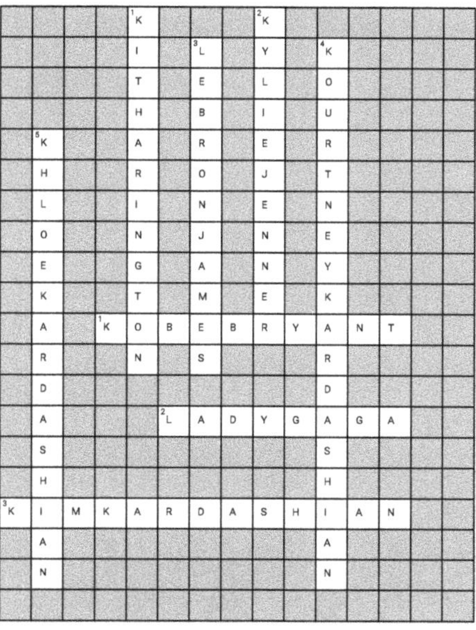

Puzzle 10

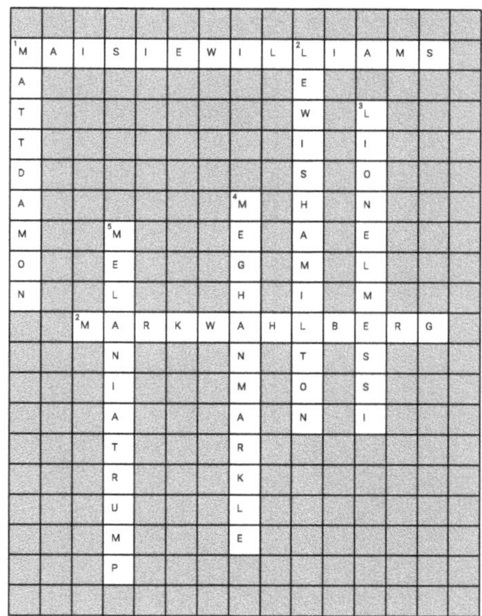

Puzzle 11

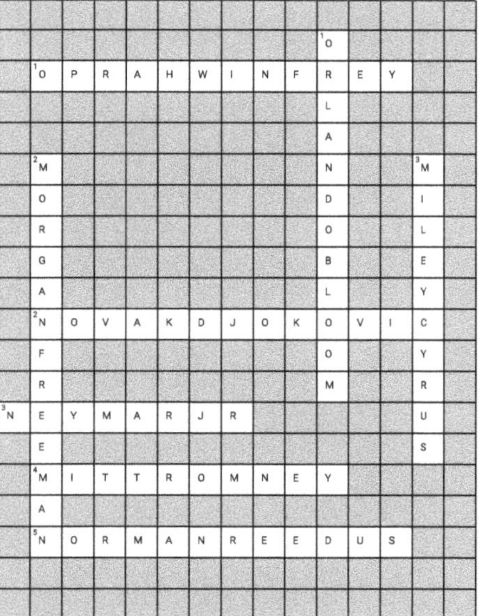

Puzzle 12

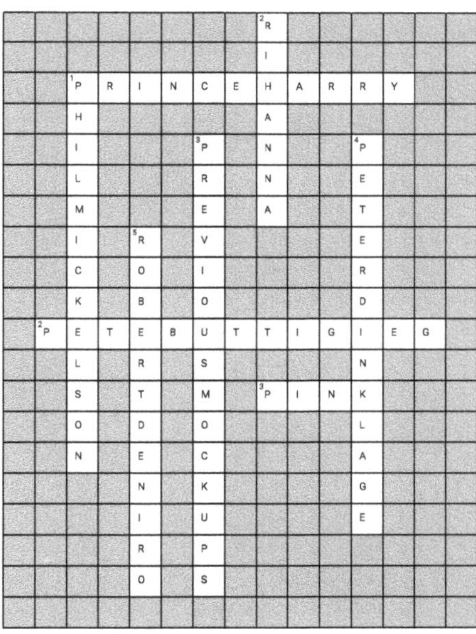

Puzzle 13

	1R	O	G	E	R	F	E	D	E	1R	E	R		
										O				
										B				
										E				
		2R	O	R	Y	M	C	I	L	R	O	Y		
										T				
					2R			3R		P				
					O			Y		A				
					B			A		T				
					I			N		T				
		3R	Y	A	N	G	O	S	L	I	N	G		
					W			E		N				
					I			A		S				
					L			C		O				
4R	U	S	S	E	L	L	B	R	A	N	D			
					I			E						
					A			S						
					M			T						
					S									

Puzzle 14

			1S	I	M	O	N	C	O	W	E	L	L	
			C											
	2S	H	A	W	N	M	E	N	D	E	S			
			R											
			L											
	3S	T	E	P	H	E	N	K	I	N	G			
			T											
		4S	T	E	P	H	E	N	C	U	R	R	Y	
			J											
		5S	O	F	I	A	V	E	R	G	A	R	A	
			H											
	6S	E	A	N	C	O	M	B	S					
			N											
			S											
			7S	E	L	E	N	A	G	O	M	E	Z	
			O											
			N											

Puzzle 15

		4S		2S								3S		
		Y		T								T		
		L		E								E		
		V		V								V		
1T	H	E	W	E	E	K	N	D				E		
I		S		N						5T		H		
G		T		S		6T				A		A		
E		E		P		O				Y		R		
R		R		I		M				L		V		
W		3S	T	E	P	H	E	N	M	O	Y	E	R	
O		T		L		A				R		Y		
O		A		B		N				S				
D		L		E		K				W				
S		L		R		S				I				
		O		G						F				
		N								T				
		E												

www.ingramcontent.com/pod-product-compliance
Lightning Source LLC
Chambersburg PA
CBHW080206300326
41934CB00038B/3389
* 9 7 9 8 8 8 7 0 0 6 0 9 3 *